one-stop
science

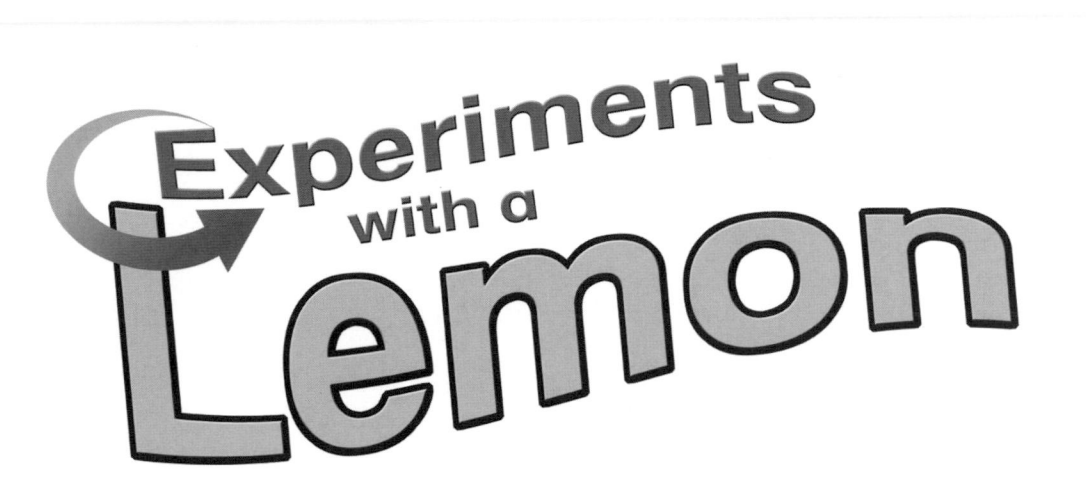

Experiments
with a
Lemon

By Angela Royston

Smart Apple Media

Published by Smart Apple Media,
an imprint of Black Rabbit Books
P.O. Box 3263, Mankato, Minnesota 56002
www.smartapplemedia.com

Cataloging-in-Publication Data is available from
the Library of Congress
ISBN: 978-1-62588-140-3 (library binding)
ISBN: 978-1-68071-015-1 (eBook)

Series editor: Sarah Peutrill
Art director: Jonathan Hair
Design: Matt Lilly and Ruth Walton
Science consultant: Meredith Blakeney
Models: Rianna Aniakor, Dilvinder Dilan
Bhamra, Brandon Ford, Yusuf Hofri and
India May Nugent
Photography: Paul Bricknell, unless
otherwise stated

Published by arrangement with Franklin Watts,
London.

Printed in the United States of America by CG
Book Printers, North Mankato, Minnesota.

PO1777
3-2016

Contents

Words in **bold** are in the glossary on page 28.

What is a Lemon?

A lemon is the fruit of a lemon tree. Lemons have a strong smell and a strong taste.

Lemons are used to flavor food, such as lemon sorbet and lemon meringue pie, and the juice is often squeezed over fish and into salad dressings. Lemons have a clean, fresh smell. They are used to scent soaps, shampoos, dish soap, and other household products.

▲ Lemon juice is used to flavor the fish and the cake, and it makes the dish soap smell fresh.

Lemon trees

Lemons, oranges, grapefruit, and limes are different kinds of citrus fruits. Citrus trees grow between 16–50 feet (5–15 m) tall and have sharp spines along their twigs. They are **evergreens** and grow best in hot places. They flower in spring, and the fruit grows and ripens during summer and autumn.

◄ The fruit from the previous year may still be on the tree when the flowers open.

Examine a Lemon

You will need:
A lemon
A knife
A plate or cutting board
A teaspoon

Rind

Flesh

1

Cut a lemon in half. Look for the outer rind and the white pith. The pips are the seeds. Look for them inside the juicy flesh.

Pith

Seed

2

Smell the rind and the flesh. Which smells stronger?

3

Put some of the flesh onto a clean teaspoon and taste it. Is it sweet, salty, sour, or bitter?

Growing a Lemon Tree

Plant some lemon seeds and watch them grow into small plants. It may take several weeks before the seeds begin to grow, so you will have to be patient!

You will need:
3 or 4 lemon seeds
A clear plastic cup
A corkscrew or large
    screw or nail
Potting soil (see Tip)
A saucer
Water
Squared paper, a ruler, and pencil

1

Soak the seeds in water for a few days. Make several holes with the corkscrew in the bottom of the cup. Ask an adult to help you.

2 Fill the cup about two thirds full with compost. Water the compost well. Plant the seeds by pushing them about 0.4–0.8 inches (1–2 cm) into the soil around the edge of the cup. Make sure you can see the seeds through the side of the cup.

Seed

Tip:

The lemon seeds will grow best in acidic (lime-free) soil. You can buy it from a garden store.

3

Put the cup in a warm place, on a sunny windowsill, or near a radiator. Water the seeds every few days and wait.

4 Watch carefully. When the seeds begin to sprout they will grow quite fast. Which part of the plant grows first?

5

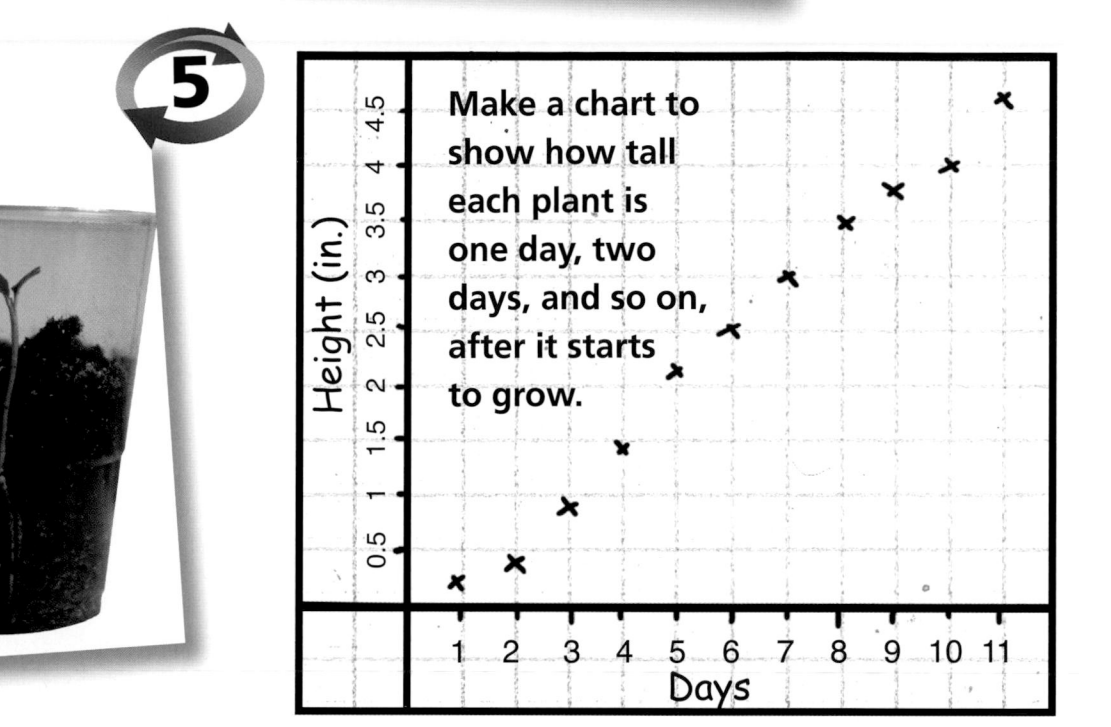

Make a chart to show how tall each plant is one day, two days, and so on, after it starts to grow.

Height (in.)

0.5 1 1.5 2 2.5 3 3.5 4 4.5

1 2 3 4 5 6 7 8 9 10 11

Days

What happened?

A seed begins to grow when it is warm and damp. At first the tiny plant used the store of food inside the seed itself. Then the roots took in water and **nutrients** from the soil or compost. The leaves made food for the plant.

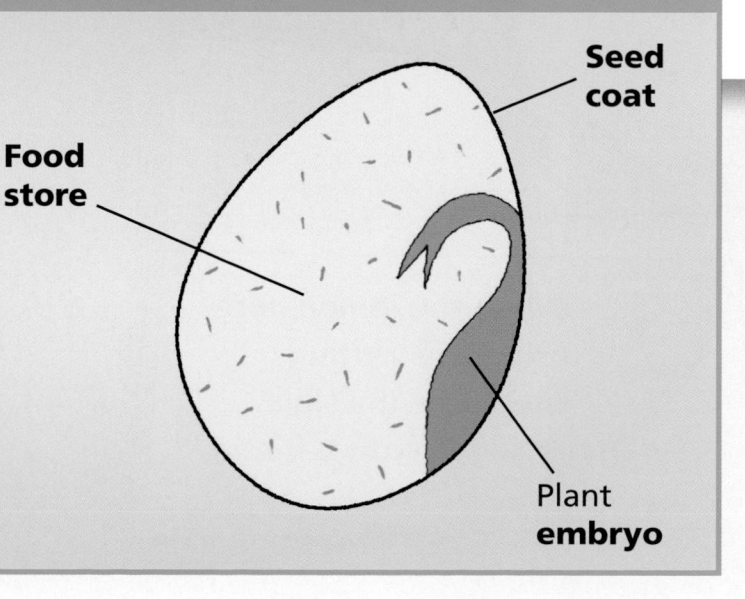

Seed coat

Food store

Plant **embryo**

Invisible Ink

Lemon juice makes good invisible ink. Use it to write secret notes to your friends or to record secret thoughts in your diary.

You will need:
A lemon
A knife
A lemon juicer
A paintbrush
A piece of paper
A toaster

1 Cut the lemon in half around the middle and squeeze out the juice.

2 Dip the paintbrush into the juice and use it to write a message or draw a picture on the paper.

3 When the lemon juice dries, the writing should be invisible. Swap messages with a friend.

4 To read the message, hold the paper above a hot toaster. The paper must not touch the toaster. As the heat reaches the writing, the message should slowly appear.

Make sure an adult is close by when you do this activity.

What happened?

Lemon juice is a mixture of water and other substances, including **carbon**. The writing dried when the water **evaporated**, leaving behind the carbon. When you heated the paper, the carbon burned and turned brown. This revealed the picture or writing!

Blow Up a Balloon

How can you blow up a balloon without blowing or pumping air into it? **By using lemon juice!**

You will need:
A balloon
A lemon
A knife
A lemon juicer
A funnel
1 teaspoon of baking soda
A jug

1 Cut the lemon in half and squeeze out the juice.

2 Stretch the end of the balloon over the end of the funnel.

3 Pour in the lemon juice.

4 Add the baking soda and then quickly take out the funnel and knot the end of the balloon. Now watch what happens.

What happens?

The baking soda **reacts** with the lemon juice to form new substances. One of the substances is the gas **carbon dioxide**. The gas fills the balloon. The more gas there is, the bigger the balloon becomes.

Making Bubbles

If you want to see the carbon dioxide, then try this experiment.

You will need:
Juice from a lemon
A jug
Dish soap
A large clear plastic cup
1 teaspoon of baking soda
A teaspoon

1 Put the baking soda into the cup.

2 Add a squirt of dish soap and mix the two together.

3 Add the lemon juice and watch what happens. The bubbles are carbon dioxide trapped in a thin film of dish soap.

Fizzy Lemonade

You can make your own fizzy lemonade using lemon juice and baking soda, but you have to drink it quickly before the bubbles disappear. Wash your hands before you start.

You will need:
Juice of a lemon
Water
A plastic cup
1 teaspoon of sugar
1 teaspoon of baking soda

1 Pour the juice into the cup.

2 Fill the cup with water and stir in a teaspoon of sugar.

3 Stir in a teaspoon of baking soda. What happens?

4 Drink your lemonade. What does it taste like?

All fizzy drinks contain bubbles of carbon dioxide. The carbon dioxide is added to the drink. Then the can or bottle is sealed so that the carbon dioxide cannot escape.

Lemon Drop Candy

You can make some lemon drops to go with the lemonade.

You will need:
3.5 ounces (100 g) of sugar
Juice of a lemon
A teaspoon
A non-stick baking sheet
A saucepan

1 Add the lemon juice to the sugar and stir until all the sugar has dissolved.

2 Pour the mixture into a saucepan. Ask an adult to boil it until it forms a thick syrup or until it begins to darken in color.

3 Remove from the heat. Make lemon drops by carefully spooning small spoonfuls of the syrup onto a non-stick baking sheet.

4 They are ready to eat when they have cooled and hardened.

Make Litmus Paper

Food that contains acid often tastes sour. Do you think that is why lemons taste sour? Find out by making your own litmus paper and using it to test lemon juice.

You will need:
Half a red cabbage
A food grater
A saucepan
Water
A strainer
A bowl
A coffee filter
Scissors
Juice of a lemon

1 Grate the cabbage and put it in the pan.

2 Cover with water and ask an adult to simmer it for about 15–20 minutes, until the liquid goes dark purple.

3 Strain the liquid into a bowl and leave it to cool.

4 Soak the coffee filter in the liquid. Take it out of the liquid and leave it to dry. The filter should now be purple.

5 Cut it into strips.

6 Dip one strip of paper into the lemon juice. What happens to the color?

Acids
Litmus paper turns red or pink when it soaks up an acid. Acids include vinegar and soda, as well as lemon juice. These are weak acids. Some acids, such as sulphuric acid, are very strong. Strong acids are dangerous—they are poisonous and will burn skin.

Acids and alkalis
Alkalis are the opposite of acids. They include baking soda and toothpaste. An alkali turns purple litmus paper blue or green.

The Litmus Test

Now you can use your own litmus paper (from pages 16–17) to explore what happens when you mix lemon juice with an alkali.

You will need:
Several strips of litmus paper
1 cup of water
1 teaspoon of baking soda
Juice of a lemon in a cup
Paper and pencil

1 Dip one of the strips of litmus paper into the cup of water. What happens to the color of the paper?

2 Stir the teaspoon of baking soda into the water. Test the liquid with a new strip and make a note of the color.

3 Add the lemon juice to the baking soda a little at a time. Test the mixture with a new piece of litmus paper each time. What happens as you add the acid?

Can you make a mixture that is neither acid nor alkali?

4 Make a chart and fill in your results.

Liquid	Lemon juice	Water	Water and baking soda	Mixture of lemon juice and baking soda
Color of litmus paper after test				

What happened?

Water is neither an acid nor an alkali, so the litmus paper stayed purple. Baking soda is an alkali, so it turned the litmus paper blue or green. When you mixed baking soda with lemon juice, they started to cancel each other out. The alkali is said to **neutralize** the acid.

Make Coins Shine

You can use the acid in lemon juice to clean pennies.

You will need:
Juice of a lemon in a jug
A plastic plate
Pennies that have
   lost their shine

1 Put the coins onto the plate.

2 Pour the lemon juice over the coins and leave them for 3 to 4 hours.

3 What happens to the coins?

What happened?

The **copper** on the surface of the coin combined with oxygen in the air to make **copper oxide**. This made the coin look dull. The acid in the lemon juice reacted with the copper oxide and removed it.

Turning Milk Sour

You can turn milk sour by adding lemon juice to it.

You will need:
A clear plastic cup about a quarter filled with milk
Juice of a lemon
A teaspoon

1

Add the lemon to the milk drop by drop and watch what happens.

2

Taste a sip of the milk. Is it sour?

3

Stir the milk. Can you make it smooth again?

What happened?

The acid in the lemon juice turned the milk sour. The **protein** in the milk clumped together, forming small lumps that separated from the rest of the milk. This is called curdling. You cannot stop the curdling by stirring the milk.

Disappearing Eggshell

Acids often work slowly, but they can have a powerful effect. These two experiments show you what the acid in lemon juice can do.

2 Cover the bowl and leave it for three days.

1

Put the eggshell in the bowl and pour the juice over it.

3 What happens to the eggshell? How long does it take for the eggshell to disappear?

What happened?

Eggshells contain **calcium carbonate** (chalk). The acid in the lemon juice **dissolved** the calcium carbonate. The carbonate became carbon dioxide and the **calcium** floated away. If you look carefully, you can see that the lemon juice looks slightly milky.

Acid rain

Pollution from power plants and factories combines with water vapor in the air, making the rain slightly acid. Acid rain acts on buildings and statues, particularly those made of soft stone such as limestone and sandstone, like the lemon juice acts on the eggshell. Over several years, acid rain slowly dissolves the stone. This is called erosion.

▶ The face of this statue has been eroded by acid rain.

The Chicken Bone Experiment

Repeat the eggshell experiment, but this time soak a chicken bone in lemon juice for three to five days. One of the small bones from the wing works well. What do you think will happen to the bone? Were you right?

What happened?

Like eggshell, bones contain calcium. Calcium is what makes them hard. The lemon juice dissolved the calcium, so the bone became bendy.

Make a Lemon Battery

You can use a lemon to generate a small amount of electricity. Using two lemons creates a stronger electric current.

You will need:
2 lemons
2 galvanized nails
Copper wire
Wire cutters
A small bulb
Electric wires

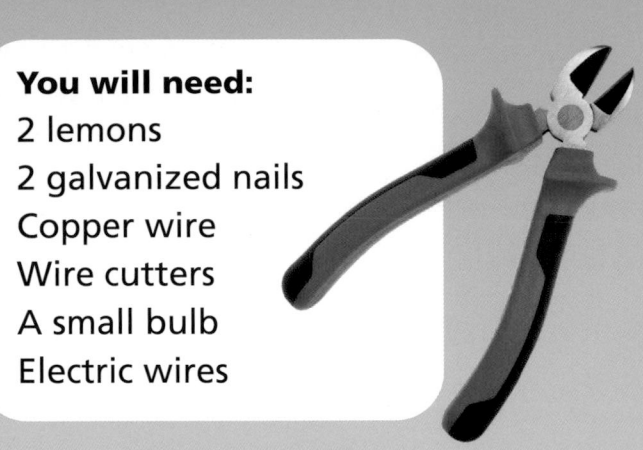

1 Shake the lemons to loosen up the lemon juice inside.

2 Stick one nail into the side of one lemon.

3 Use the wire cutters to cut about 1.6 inches (4 cm) of copper wire. Bend the wire to form a hook, and stick it into the other side of the lemon.

4 The nail and the hook are the **electrodes**. Join a piece of electric wire to each electrode.

5 Join the other ends of the wires to the bulb. The bulb should light up.

6

Make a second lemon **battery**. Join the copper hook of one battery to the nail of the other battery. Is the bulb brighter now?

What happened?

The galvanized nail is coated in **zinc**. The zinc reacted with the acidic lemon juice to produce electricity and hydrogen gas. Did you see the gas bubbling around the electrode? The copper hook conducted the electricity from the lemon into the wire.

Using the Lemon Battery

You can use your lemon battery (from pages 24–25) to work any gadget that does not need a lot of power, such as a digital clock.

You will need:
A lemon battery powered by 2 lemons (see pages 24–25)
2 pieces of copper wire, each about 8 inches (20 cm) long
A digital clock that uses one AA battery

1 Take the AA battery out of the clock. What happens to the time on the clock?

2 Look inside the clock for two **terminals**. The positive terminal is labeled with a plus (+) and the negative terminal is labeled with a minus (−).

3 Connect one of the copper wires to the zinc nail. Connect the other end to the negative terminal in the clock. Make sure all the contacts are held firmly together.

Tip:

Do not use more than two lemons in the battery. More lemons would generate too much electricity and damage the clock.

4 Use the other wire to connect the copper hook on the second lemon to the positive terminal in the clock. If necessary, use a piece of modeling clay to keep the wires in contact with the terminals.

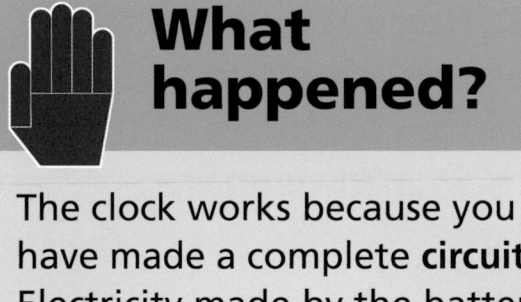

5 The clock should now work again!

What happened?

The clock works because you have made a complete **circuit**. Electricity made by the battery flows through the clock and back to the battery. You can draw the circuit as a diagram, using the symbols shown here.

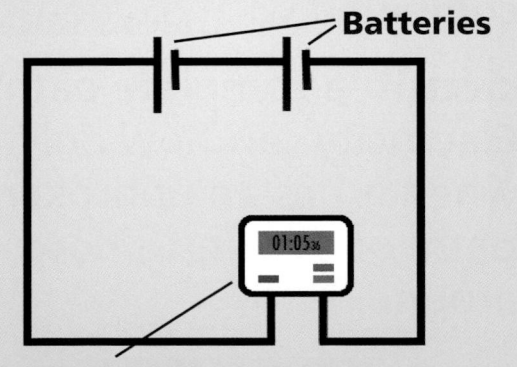

Batteries

Digital clock

Glossary

battery a device that makes a small amount of electricity when it is connected in a circuit.

calcium a chemical substance. Chalk, eggshell, bones, and teeth are just some of the things that contain calcium.

calcium carbonate a substance formed when calcium combines with carbon and oxygen.

carbon a chemical substance that is found in all plants and animals.

carbon dioxide a gas that consists of carbon combined with oxygen.

circuit a complete path. Electricity can flow only when it has an unbroken path, or circuit, to flow around.

copper a metal.

copper oxide a mixture of the metal copper and the gas oxygen.

dissolve to mix a solid with a liquid by breaking it up into tiny particles that are too small to see.

electrode a piece of metal around which chemicals collect, producing electricity.

embryo a tiny plant in a seed before it begins to grow.

evaporate to change from a liquid into a gas.

evergreen having green leaves all year round. Evergreen shrubs and trees lose their leaves gradually during the year.

neutralize to change so that a liquid is neither acid nor alkali.

nutrients substances in soil that help plants grow.

protein one of the substances that forms part of living things. Protein consists of nitrogen, carbon, hydrogen, and oxygen combined together.

react to change chemically. When two substances react they change into different substances.

terminal a piece of metal that joins a battery to an electrical circuit.

zinc a metal.

Further information

Websites

chemistry.about.com/cs/howtos/ht/buildavolcano.htm
This website tells you how to use the reaction between vinegar (or lemon juice) and baking soda to make an active volcano.

www.epa.gov/acidrain/education/experiment2.html
Ideas for experiments in which you can use litmus paper to measure the acidity of different fruits and other food.

Note to parents and teachers: The publisher has made every effort to ensure that these websites are suitable for children. However, due to the nature of the Internet, we strongly advise the supervision of web access by a responsible adult.

Books

The Kid's Book of Simple Everyday Science by Kelly Doudna, Scarletta Publishing, 2013

Slimy Science and Awesome Experiments by Susan Martineau and Martin Ursell, b small publishing, 2014

Think Like a Scientist in the Kitchen (Science Explorer Junior) by Matt Mullins, Cherry Lake Publishing, 2011

Index